The

Delicious

Chip Dip

Cookbook

About the Author

Laura Sommers is **The Recipe Lady!**

She is a loving wife and mother who lives on a small farm in Baltimore County, Maryland and has a passion for all things domestic especially when it comes to saving money. She has a profitable eBay business and is a couponing addict. Follow her tips and tricks to learn how to make delicious meals on a budget, save money or to learn the latest life hack!

Visit her Amazon Author Page to see her latest books:

amazon.com/author/laurasommers

Visit the Recipe Lady's blog for even more great recipes and to learn which books are **FREE** for download each week:

http://the-recipe-lady.blogspot.com/

Follow the Recipe Lady on **Pinterest**:

http://pinterest.com/therecipelady1

Subscribe to The Recipe Lady blog through Amazon and have recipes and updates sent directly to your Kindle:

The Recipe Lady Blog through Amazon

Laura Sommers is also an Extreme Couponer and Penny Hauler! If you would like to find out how to get things for **FREE** with coupons or how to get things for only a **PENNY**, then visit her couponing blog **Penny Items and Freebies**

http://penny-items-and-freebies.blogspot.com/

Introduction

Who doesn't love chips and dips! You can't have a party without it! But why serve the same old boring stuff when there are so many options available out there. This cookbook contains so many delicious mouth-watering dip recipes, not just for chips but also for fruit, pretzels or veggies. So for your next party, barbecue, picnic, gathering or soirée be sure to try some of these many options and it will be a hit!

Seven Layer Bean Dip

Ingredients
1 (1 oz.) pkg. taco seasoning mix
1 (16 oz.) can refried beans
1 (16 oz.) container sour cream
1 cup chunky salsa
1 large tomato, chopped
1 bunch chopped green onions
1 small head iceberg lettuce, shredded
1 (6 oz.) can sliced black olives, drained
2 cups shredded Cheddar cheese
1 cup of guacamole (package or use the guacamole recipe below)

Directions:

1. In a medium bowl, blend the taco seasoning mix and refried beans.
2. Spread the mixture onto a large serving platter.
3. Spread the guacamole over the beans
4. Spread the sour cream over the refried beans.
5. Top the layers with salsa. Place a layer of tomato, green bell pepper, green onions and lettuce over the salsa, and top with Cheddar cheese.
6. Garnish with black olives.
7. Serve and enjoy!

Guacamole

Ingredients:

3 avocados - peeled, pitted, and mashed
1 lime, juiced
1 tsp. salt
1/2 cup diced onion
3 tbsps. chopped fresh cilantro
2 Roma (plum) tomatoes, diced
1 tsp. minced garlic
1 pinch ground cayenne pepper

Directions:

1. In a medium bowl, mash together the avocados, lime juice, and salt.
2. Mix in onion, cilantro, tomatoes, and garlic.
3. Stir in cayenne pepper.
4. Refrigerate 1 hour before serving.
5. Serve and enjoy!

Mango Salsa

Ingredients:

1 mango
1/4 cup finely chopped red bell pepper
1 green onion, chopped
2 tbsps. chopped cilantro
1 fresh jalapeno chili pepper, finely chopped
2 tbsps. lime juice
1 tbsp. lemon juice

Directions:

1. Peel, seed and chop the mango.
2. In a medium bowl, mix mango, red bell pepper, green onion, cilantro, jalapeno, lime juice, and lemon juice.
3. Cover.
4. Let it sit for at least 30 minutes before serving.
5. Serve and enjoy!

Pico de Galo

Ingredients:

1 pound tomatoes (4 plum or 2 beefsteak)
1 jalapeno
1/2 white onion, finely chopped
1/4 cup fresh cilantro, chopped
1 tbsp. fresh lime juice
1/2 tsp. kosher salt
1/4 tsp. black pepper

Directions:

1. Seed and chop the tomatoes.
1. Chop the jalapenos and seed for less heat if desired.
2. Combine all the ingredients in a bowl.
3. Toss.
4. Chill.
5. Serve and enjoy!

Sour Cream and

Onion Dip

Ingredients:

1/4 cup extra-virgin olive oil
1 (1-pound) large onion, chopped (3 cups)
1/2 pound shallots, chopped (1 1/2 cups)
Salt
Freshly ground black pepper
4 tbsps. water
1 (16-oz.) container sour cream
1/4 cup chopped chives or finely chopped scallion greens

Directions:

1. Heat oil in a 12-inch heavy skillet over medium-high heat until it shimmers.
2. Sauté the onion and shallots with 1 tsp. salt until lightly browned, about 2 minutes.
3. Reduce heat to medium-low and continue to cook, covered, stirring frequently, until vegetables are golden brown (about 20 to 30 minutes more).
4. 4. Remove from heat and stir in 1/4 tsp. pepper and 2 tbsps. water, or enough to loosen any brown bits stuck to the bottom of the skillet.
5. Transfer onion mixture to a medium bowl, then stir in sour cream and remaining 2 tbsps. water.
6. Stir in most of the chives, sprinkling on the rest as a garnish.
7. Serve and enjoy!

Dill Dip (In a Bread Bowl)

Ingredients:

1 cup mayonnaise
1 cup sour cream
1 garlic clove, minced
1 tbsp. dill weed
1 tbsp. shallot, minced
1 tbsp. minced fresh parsley leaves
1 tbsp. seasoning salt
2 round dill or onion bread loaves

Directions:

1. Mix all of the ingredients together in a medium bowl.
2. Cut out the center of 1 bread round and mound dill dip into the interior cavity of the bread bowl.
3. Cut up other bread round into 2-inch squares and dip bread into bowl.
4. Serve and enjoy!

Spinach and Artichoke Dip

Ingredients:

1 (14 oz.) can artichoke hearts, drained and chopped
1 (10 oz.) pkg. frozen chopped spinach, thawed and drained
1 cup mayonnaise
1 cup grated Parmesan cheese
2 1/2 cups shredded Monterey Jack cheese

Directions:

1. Preheat oven to 350 degrees F (175 degrees C). Lightly grease a 1 quart baking dish.
2. In a medium bowl, mix together artichoke hearts, spinach, mayonnaise, Parmesan cheese and 2 cups Monterey Jack cheese.
3. Transfer mixture to the prepared baking dish, and sprinkle with remaining 1/2 cup of Monterey Jack cheese.
4. Bake in the center of the preheated oven until the cheese is melted, about 15 minutes.
5. Serve and enjoy!

Caramel Apple Dip

Ingredients:

1 pkg. (8 oz.) cream cheese, softened
1/2 cup packed brown sugar
1/2 tsp. vanilla

Directions:

1. Beat cream cheese in small bowl with mixer until creamy.
2. Add sugar and vanilla.
3. Mix well.
4. Serve and enjoy!

Pizza Dip

Ingredients:

1 (14 oz.) jar pizza sauce
1 cup chopped pepperoni
1/2 cup green onions, chopped
1/2 cup chopped red bell pepper
1 can (2 1/4 oz.) sliced ripe olives, drained
1 cup shredded mozzarella cheese (4 oz.)
1 (8 oz.) pkg. cream cheese, cut into cubes
Broccoli florets, cherry tomatoes and carrot sticks

Directions:

1. Spray 1 1/2-quart slow cooker with cooking spray.
2. In slow cooker, mix pizza sauce, pepperoni, onions, bell pepper and olives.
3. Cover.
4. Cook on Low heat setting for 3 to 4 hours.
5. Add mozzarella cheese and cream cheese to dip.
6. Stir until melted.
7. Serve and enjoy!

Buffalo Chicken Dip

Ingredients:

2 cups shredded cooked chicken
1 (8 oz.) pkg. cream cheese, softened
1/2 cup buffalo wing sauce
1/2 cup blue cheese or ranch dressing
1/2 cup crumbled bleu cheese

Directions:

1. Preheat oven to 350 degrees.
1. Combine all ingredients and spoon into shallow 1-quart baking dish.
2. Bake 20 minutes or until mixture is heated through.
3. Stir.
4. Garnish with chopped green onions if desired.
5. Serve with crackers or vegetables and enjoy!

Maryland Crab Dip

Ingredients:

1 (8 oz.) pkg. cream cheese softened
1 cup mayonnaise
2 tsps. Old Bay Seasoning
1/2 tsp. ground mustard
1 pound lump crabmeat (preferably Chesapeake Bay blue crab)
1/4 cup cheddar cheese shredded
Crackers or sliced French bread

Directions:

1. Preheat oven to 350 degrees F.
1. In a medium bowl, mix cream cheese, mayonnaise, Old Bay seasoning and ground mustard until well blended.
2. Add crabmeat.
3. Toss gently.
4. Spread in a 9-inch pie plate.
5. Sprinkle with cheddar cheese and additional Old Bay seasoning.
6. Bake 30 minutes or until hot and bubbly.
7. Serve with assorted crackers or sliced French bread and enjoy!

Queso Cabeza Dip

Ingredients:

1 pound lean ground beef
1 (1 oz.) pkg. taco seasoning mix
¼ cup water
10 oz. cream cheese, cut into 2-inch cubes
1 1/2 cups thick and chunky salsa
2 cans (4.5 oz. each) chopped green chilies
2 cups shredded cheddar cheese (8 oz.)
Tortilla chips for dipping.

Directions:

1. In a large skillet, brown the beef until thoroughly cooked.
2. Drain.
3. Sprinkle with taco seasoning mix and water.
4. Stir.
5. In a 4-quart saucepan, heat cream cheese and salsa over medium heat.
6. Stir occasionally for 4 to 5 minutes, or until mixture is lump-free.
7. Stir in chilies, cheese and beef.
8. Continue cooking about 5 minutes, stirring occasionally, until cheese is melted and mixture is hot.
9. Serve and enjoy!

Bacon and Swiss Cheese Dip

Ingredients:

8 slices bacon
8 oz. softened cream cheese
1/2 cup mayonnaise
2 rounded tsps. prepared Dijon style mustard
1 1/2 cups shredded Swiss cheese
3 scallions, chopped
1/2 cup smoked almonds, coarsely chopped
Ingredients for dipping such as baby carrots and breads (cocktail sized
Pumpernickel or rye, or sliced whole grain baguettes)

Directions:

1. Preheat oven to 400 degrees.
2. Cook bacon until crisp.
3. Lay bacon on paper towels to drain.
4. Crumble bacon in to bits.
5. In a mixing bowl, combine cream cheese, mayonnaise, Dijon, Swiss and scallions with cooked bacon.
6. Transfer to a shallow small casserole or baking dish and bake until golden and bubbly at edges, 15 to 18 minutes.
7. Top with chopped smoked almonds.
8. Place dip on a platter and surround warm casserole with breads and carrots for dipping.
9. For a variation, stir in 2 rounded tsps. prepared horseradish when
10. combining cheese and bacon
11. Serve and enjoy!

Pepper Jelly Dip

Ingredients:

1 pkg. of cream cheese (softened)
1 jar of pepper jelly (I usually get this from Williams-Sonoma)

Directions:

1. Put pepper jelly and cream cheese in a mixer
2. Mix until well blended.
3. Serve and enjoy!

Pumpkin Pie Dip

Ingredients:

1 (8 oz.) pkg. spreadable cream cheese, room temperature
1 cup canned pumpkin
3/4 cup powdered sugar
1 1/2 tsp. pumpkin pie spice
1 tsp. cinnamon
1/2 tsp. vanilla
1/2 container non-dairy whipped topping

Directions:

1. Mix together all of the ingredients and blend until smooth in a mixer.
2. Chill in the refrigerator.
3. Serve cold, with graham crackers, fruit, cinnamon pita chips, or
4. vanilla wafers
5. Serve and enjoy!

Cherry Cheesecake Dip

Ingredients:

8 oz. Greek yogurt cream cheese, softened
10 oz. non-dairy whipped topping
1 cup plain, nonfat Greek yogurt
1/2 cup fat-free sweetened condensed milk
1 (21 oz.) can cherry pie filling

Directions:

1. Beat together cream cheese and nondairy whipped topping until well blended.
2. Mix in Greek yogurt and sweetened condensed milk until blended.
3. Spread into a dish.
4. Top with pie filling.
5. Chill until ready to serve.
6. Serve with graham crackers, vanilla wafers, pretzels, or other desired dippers and enjoy!

Strawberry Cheesecake Dip

Ingredients:

8 oz. cream cheese
2/3 cup powdered sugar
1/2 cup sour cream
Pinch of salt
2 1/2 cups strawberries, pureed, plus 1/2 cup chopped strawberries
3/4 cup heavy cream
Graham crackers, for serving

Directions:

1. Using a hand or stand mixer, blend together cream cheese, powdered sugar, sour cream, and salt until well combined.
2. Fold in strawberry puree and pour into a mixing bowl.
3. Set aside.
4. Beat cream until stiff peaks form, about 3 minutes.
5. Fold cream into cream cheese mixture.
6. Chill in the refrigerator to thicken at least 45 minutes.
7. Serve and enjoy!

Philly Cheesesteak Dip

Ingredients:

2 tsps. vegetable oil
1/2 cup chopped onion
1 cup chopped red and green bell pepper
1/2 pound sliced roast beef, chopped
1 can (4.5 oz.) green chilies
8 slices white American cheese cut into pieces
1 (3oz.) pkg. cream cheese
1/4 cup mayonnaise
1/8 tsp. pepper
1/4 cup grated Parmesan cheese
Hard sourdough pretzels for dipping

Directions:

1. Heat oven to 350 degrees.
2. Lightly spray ovenproof 1-quart baking dish with cooking spray.
3. In 10-inch skillet, heat oil, onion and bell peppers over medium heat.
4. Cook and stir about 5 minutes or until onion has softened and turned translucent.
5. Stir in roast beef; cook 2 minutes. Add chilies, American cheese, cream cheese, mayonnaise and pepper; stir until cheese is melted.
6. Pour mixture into baking dish; sprinkle with Parmesan cheese.
7. Bake uncovered 25 to 30 minutes or until golden brown on top.
8. Serve with pretzels and enjoy!

Fluffernutter Dip

Ingredients:

1/2 small jar marshmallow cream
1/2 cup peanut butter
1 tbsp. lemon juice
Water

Directions:

1. Mix marshmallow cream, peanut butter and lemon juice until smooth.
2. Add a little of water if mixture is too thick to easily mix.
3. Chill for 30 minutes before serving.
4. Serve with fruit or graham crackers and enjoy!

Pimiento Cheese Dip

Ingredients:

2 cups sharp yellow cheddar cheese
2 cups extra-sharp white cheddar cheese, coarsely grated
1 cup drained pimentos or roasted red peppers, finely chopped
1/2 cup mayonnaise
1/2 tsp. celery salt
  Salt and freshly ground pepper
Serve with crackers, baguette slices, assorted raw vegetables

Directions:

1. Mix all ingredients in large bowl.
2. Season with salt and pepper to taste.
3. Cover and chill.
4. Serve with crackers, baguette slices, and vegetables and enjoy!

Key Lime Pie Dip

Ingredients
2 (8-oz) blocks of cream cheese, softened
½ cup key lime juice
1 (14-oz) can condensed milk
¼ cup sugar

Directions:

1. Whip together cream cheese until smooth using an electric mixer on medium speed.
2. Add in lime juice and sugar and mix together.
3. Add condensed milk.
4. Mix until smooth.
5. Cover and refrigerate for at least 1 hour.
6. Serve and enjoy!

Tapenade

Ingredients:

1 cup Kalamata or Nicoise olives, pitted
1 clove garlic, peeled
1 tbsp. capers, drained and rinsed
3 oil-cured anchovy fillets
Freshly ground pepper, to taste
2 tbsps. chopped parsley
2 tbsps. extra-virgin olive oil

Directions:

1. Coarsely chop olives garlic, capers and anchovies.
1. Place mixture in a bowl.
2. Add pepper and parsley.
3. Stir in olive oil.
4. Chill.
5. Serve and enjoy!

Nacho Chicken Dip

Ingredients:

1 (14 oz.) can diced tomatoes with green chile peppers, drained
1 (1 pound) block processed cheese food, cubed
2 large cooked skinless, boneless chicken breast halves, shredded
1/3 cup sour cream
1/4 cup diced green onion
1 1/2 tbsps. taco seasoning mix
2 tbsps. minced jalapeno pepper, or to taste (optional)
1 cup black beans, rinsed and drained

Directions:

1. Place the diced tomatoes, processed cheese, chicken meat, sour cream, green onion, taco seasoning, and jalapeno pepper into a slow cooker.
2. Cook on High, stirring occasionally until the cheese has melted and the dip is hot, 1 to 2 hours.
3. Stir in the black beans, and cook 15 more minutes to reheat.
4. Serve and enjoy!

Reuben Dip

Ingredients:

1/2 cup mayonnaise
1/2 cup Thousand Island dressing
16 oz. sauerkraut, rinsed and squeezed dry
8 oz. shredded corned beef
16 oz. shredded Swiss cheese

Directions:

1. Preheat oven to 350 degrees F (175 degrees C).
2. In a small bowl, combine mayonnaise and dressing.
3. Spread sauerkraut into a 9x13-inch baking dish.
4. Layer corned beef, Swiss cheese, and the mayonnaise-dressing mixture on top of the sauerkraut.
5. Bake for 20 to 25 minutes.
6. Serve and enjoy!

Cheddar Ranch Dip

Ingredients:

1 (16 oz.) container sour cream
1 (1 oz.) pkg. dry Ranch-style dressing mix
1 (3 oz.) can bacon bits
1 cup shredded Cheddar cheese

Directions:

1. In a medium bowl, thoroughly blend the sour cream and ranch-style dressing mix.
2. Mix in the bacon bits and Cheddar cheese.
3. Chill in the refrigerator 20 minutes or longer before serving.
4. Serve and enjoy!

Baked Potato Dip

Ingredients:

2 (16 oz.) containers sour cream
1 (3 oz.) can bacon bits 2 cups shredded Cheddar cheese
1 bunch green onions, chopped

Directions:

1. In a medium size mixing bowl, combine sour cream, bacon, Cheddar cheese and green onions.
2. Stir well.
3. Serve and enjoy!

BBQ Bacon Ranch Dip

Ingredients:

7 slices bacon
2 (8 oz.) pkgs. cream cheese, softened
1 (1 oz.) envelope ranch dressing mix
1/2 cup barbeque sauce
1 green bell pepper, chopped
1 tomato, chopped
1 1/2 cups shredded sharp Cheddar cheese

Directions:

1. Place the bacon in a large, deep skillet.
2. Cook over medium-high heat, turning occasionally, until evenly browned, about 10 minutes.
3. Drain the bacon slices on a paper towel-lined plate.
4. Crumble the cooled bacon into a bowl and set aside.
5. Stir together the cream cheese and ranch dressing mix in a bowl until smooth.
6. Spread the mixture on the bottom of a pie dish.
7. Evenly spread the barbecue sauce on top of the cream cheese mixture.
8. Layer the bacon, bell pepper, and tomato on top of the barbecue sauce and top with the Cheddar cheese.
9. Cover and chill for 1 hour before serving.
10. Serve and enjoy!

BLT Dip

Ingredients:

1 pound bacon
1 cup mayonnaise
1 cup sour cream
1 tomato, peeled, seeded and diced

Directions:

1. Place bacon in a large, deep skillet.
2. Cook over medium high heat until evenly brown.
3. Drain on paper towels.
4. In a medium bowl, combine mayonnaise and sour cream.
5. Crumble bacon into the sour cream and mayonnaise mixture.
6. Mix in tomatoes just before serving.
7. Serve and enjoy!

Cranberry Dip

Ingredients:

1 (12 oz.) pkg. fresh cranberries
1 cup white sugar
1 cup apricot jam
1 cup chopped pecans
1 (8 oz.) pkg. cream cheese

Directions:

1. Preheat an oven to 350 degrees F (175 degrees C).
2. Combine cranberries with sugar in a 2 quart baking dish with a lid, stirring well to coat all the berries.
3. Bake in the preheated oven, covered, for about 30 minutes, until the cranberries pop and release their liquid.
4. Remove from oven and stir in the apricot jam and pecans.
5. Refrigerate overnight to blend the flavors.
6. To serve, allow the cream cheese to come to room temperature, and pour dip over the block of cream cheese on a serving dish.
7. Serve with buttery round crackers or small pretzels and enjoy!

Cannoli Dip

2 cups ricotta cheese
1 (8 oz.) pkg. cream cheese
1 1/2 cups confectioners' sugar
1 tsp. vanilla extract 1 cup miniature semisweet chocolate chips

Directions:

1. Beat ricotta cheese and cream cheese together in a bowl until smooth.
2. Add sugar and vanilla.
3. Continue to stir mixture until sugar is completely incorporated.
4. Fold chocolate chips through the cheese mixture.
5. Cover bowl with plastic wrap and refrigerate until chilled, at least 10 minutes.
6. Serve and enjoy!

Chocolate Chip Cheesecake Dip

Ingredients:

8 oz. cream cheese, softened
1/2 cup unsalted butter, softened
3/4 cup confectioners' sugar
2 tbsps. brown sugar
1 tsp. vanilla extract
1 cup miniature semisweet chocolate chips

Directions:

1. Beat cream cheese and butter together in a bowl until smooth.
2. Add confectioners' sugar, brown sugar, and vanilla to the cheese mixture; stir.
3. Stir chocolate chips through the cheese mixture.
4. Serve and enjoy!

Cheesy Chili Dip

Ingredients:

1 (15 oz.) can chili
1 (8 oz.) pkg. cream cheese, cubed
2 (8 oz.) pkgs. shredded mozzarella cheese
Garlic powder to taste
Ground black pepper to taste

Directions:

1. Preheat the broiler.
2. In a shallow, medium baking dish, spread the chili and mix in cream cheese.
3. Microwave on high 1 minute, or until cheese is melted and creamy.
4. Stir in 1/2 the mozzarella cheese, garlic powder and pepper.
5. Microwave on high 1 minute, or until melted.
6. Top the mixture with remaining mozzarella cheese.
7. Broil 5 minutes, or until cheese is bubbly and lightly browned.
8. Serve and enjoy!

Blue Cheese Dip

Ingredients:

1 cup mayonnaise
1 cup sour cream
4 green onions, finely chopped
2 tbsps. dried parsley
4 oz. blue cheese, crumbled
Garlic salt to taste

Directions:

1. In a medium bowl, mix mayonnaise, sour cream, green onions, dried parsley, blue cheese and garlic salt.
2. Cover and chill in the refrigerator until serving.
3. Serve and enjoy!

Hot Green Chile Corn Dip

Ingredients:

1 (15.25 oz.) can whole kernel sweet corn, drained
2 (4 oz.) cans chopped green chilies, drained
1 cup shredded Monterey Jack cheese
1 cup mayonnaise
1/2 cup grated Parmesan cheese
1 (4 oz.) can chopped olives

Directions:

1. Preheat oven to 350 degrees F (175 degrees C).
2. Mix corn, green chilies, Monterey Jack cheese, mayonnaise, and Parmesan cheese in a 2-quart baking dish.
3. Bake in preheated oven until the cheese is melted and the dip is hot in the center, about 30 minutes.
4. Top with olives to serve.
5. Serve and enjoy!

Leek Dip

Ingredients:

3/4 cup chopped leeks
1 (8 oz.) pkg. cream cheese, softened
1 cup creamy salad dressing
1 tbsp. white vinegar
1 tbsp. white sugar
1/2 (12 oz.) jar bacon bits salt and pepper to taste

Directions:

1. In a medium bowl, mix together the leeks, cream cheese, creamy salad dressing, vinegar, sugar, bacon bits, salt and pepper.
2. Refrigerate 2 to 3 hours, until well chilled.
3. Serve and enjoy!

Almond Dip

Ingredients:

5 slices bacon
1 1/2 cups whole almonds, raw
8 oz. cream cheese, softened
1/2 cup mayonnaise 1 tbsp. chopped green onions
1/2 tsp. dried dill weed
Pinch of freshly ground black pepper
1 tsp. whole pine nuts (optional) crackers

Directions:

1. Place bacon in a large, deep skillet.
2. Cook over medium high heat until evenly brown. Drain, crumble, and set aside.
3. Preheat oven to 300 degrees F (150 degrees Celsius).
4. Arrange almonds on a baking sheet in a single layer.
5. Bake in the preheated oven for 15 minutes, watching carefully and stirring occasionally to prevent burning. Remove from oven, and set aside to cool.
6. In a bowl, mix together softened cream cheese, mayonnaise, green onions, crumbled bacon, dill weed, and black pepper until well blended.
7. Form mixture into a pinecone shape, and carefully place on a serving dish.
8. Beginning at the top of the "pinecone" with the points facing upward, press cooled almonds gently into cheese, each point slightly overlapping the bottom of the almond above. If desired, press a few pine nuts randomly between some of the almonds.
9. Serve and enjoy!

Avocado Leek Dip

Ingredients:

1 tbsp. olive oil
1 leek, chopped
1 avocado, peeled and pitted
1/4 cup prepared horseradish, or to taste
1 lemon, juiced salt to taste

Directions:

1. Heat olive oil in a skillet over medium heat; cook and stir leek until lightly browned, 5 to 10 minutes.
2. Add avocado and horseradish; cook, mashing avocado with a wooden spoon, until heated through, 2 to 3 minutes.
3. Stir lemon juice and salt into avocado-leek mixture.
4. Blend avocado-leek mixture in a blender until desired consistency is reached.
5. Serve and enjoy!

Garlic Bread Pizza Dip

Ingredients:

2 cup shredded mozzarella
8 oz. cream cheese, softened
1/2 cup ricotta
1/4 cup plus 1 tbsp. grated Parmesan
1 tbsp. Italian seasoning
1/2 tsp. crushed red pepper flakes
Kosher salt
1 can refrigerated biscuits (such as Pillsbury Grands)
2 tbsp. extra-virgin olive oil
3 cloves garlic, minced
1 tbsp. Freshly Chopped Parsley
1/4 cup pizza sauce or marinara

Directions:

1. Preheat oven to 375 degrees F.
2. In a large bowl combine mozzarella, cream cheese, ricotta, 1/4 cup
3. Parmesan, Italian seasoning, and crushed red pepper flakes and season with salt. Stir to combine.
4. Halve biscuits and roll into balls. Place in skillet in a ring.
5. In a small bowl, combine olive oil, garlic, and parsley.
6. Brush on biscuits.
7. Place dip inside of ring and spoon over marinara.
8. Top with remaining 3/4 cups mozzarella and mini pepperoni.
9. Sprinkle remaining tbsp. Parmesan all over.
10. Bake until biscuits are golden and cheese is melty, about 30 minutes.
11. Serve and enjoy!

Smoked Salmon Spread

Ingredients:

1 (8 oz.) pkg. cream cheese, softened
6 oz. smoked salmon, chopped
1/4 cup capers, or to taste
2 tbsps. chopped green onion (optional)
1 1/2 tsps. chopped fresh dill
1/4 cup heavy whipping cream
3 dashes Worcestershire sauce
3 drops hot pepper sauce
1 squeeze fresh lemon juice

Directions:

1. Process cream cheese in a food processor to soften completely; add salmon, capers, green onion, dill, cream, Worcestershire sauce, hot pepper sauce, and lemon juice.
2. Process the mixture again until creamy and smooth.
3. Serve and enjoy!

Beer Cheese Dip

Ingredients:

1 1/2 cup grated Cheddar, plus more for sprinkling
1/2 cup grated mozzarella
8 oz. cream cheese, softened
1 1/2 tbsp. Dijon mustard
2 tbsp. chopped chives, plus more for garnish
2 tsp. garlic powder
1/4 cup dark beer (such as Guinness)
1/4 tsp. black pepper
2 tbsp. baking soda
1 can biscuits
Egg wash, for brushing biscuits
Coarse salt, for sprinkling

Directions:

1. Preheat oven to 350 degrees F.
1. Make Beer Cheese Dip: In a large bowl, combine cheddar, mozzarella, cream cheese, Dijon, chives, garlic powder, and beer and season with salt and black pepper.
2. Make Pretzels: In a small saucepan, bring 2 cups water and baking soda to a boil.
3. Reduce to a simmer. Cut each biscuit in half and roll into a ball.
4. Slice an X across the top. Drop into simmering water with baking soda and let cook 1 minute, then remove with a slotted spoon and transfer to a cast-iron skillet, forming a ring along the inside edge.
5. Brush biscuits with egg wash and sprinkle with coarse salt.
6. Transfer cheese dip to the center of the skillet and smooth top.
7. Sprinkle with more cheddar.
8. Bake until biscuits are golden and dip is warmed through and bubbly, 30 to 35 minutes.
9. Garnish with chives and serve.
10. Serve and enjoy!

ABC Dip

Ingredients:

1/2 cup slivered almonds, toasted
1 1/4 cup mayonnaise
2 tbsp. cream cheese, softened
4 slices bacon, cooked and crumbled
1 1/2 cup shredded sharp Cheddar
2 scallions, thinly sliced
Kosher salt
Freshly ground black pepper
Pretzels, for serving

Directions:

1. In a serving bowl, combine almonds, mayonnaise, cream cheese, bacon, cheddar, and scallions.
2. Season to taste with salt and pepper.
3. Serve with pretzels.
4. Serve and enjoy!

Brownie Batter Dip

Ingredients:

1 stick butter, melted
2/3 cup sugar
1/3 cup cocoa powder
1/2 cup flour
1/4 tsp. salt
1/2 cup plain yogurt (Greek or regular)
1 bag mini M&Ms

Directions:

1. Whisk melted butter and sugar until combined. Stir in cocoa powder, flour, salt, then fold in yogurt, until no streaks of yogurt remain and any lumps in the dip are broken up.
2. Top with mini chocolate chips or M&Ms.
3. Serve with sliced apples and pretzels and enjoy!

Apple Dip

Ingredients:

1 (8 oz.) pkg. cream cheese
1/2 cup brown sugar 1 tbsp. vanilla extract

Directions:

1. Stir together the cream cheese, brown sugar, and vanilla extract until the sugar has dissolved, and the mixture is smooth.
2. Serve and enjoy!

7-Layer Greek Dip

Ingredients:

1 cup hummus
2 medium cucumbers, chopped
2 cup Kalamata olives, pitted and halved
1 can artichoke hearts, chopped
2 cup Greek yogurt
Juice of 1 lemon
2 tbsp. chopped dill
1 pt. cherry tomatoes, halved
1 cup crumbled feta
1/4 cup Chopped flat-leaf parsley
Pita chips, for serving

Directions:

1. Spread hummus evenly on the bottom of your serving dish. Top with an even layer of chopped cucumber. Spread Kalamata olives on top.
2. Make yogurt sauce. Combine yogurt, dill and lemon juice in a separate medium bowl.
3. Mix ingredients with spoon, then spread the yogurt sauce over the olive layer. Top with an even layer of cherry tomatoes, then top with crumbled feta. Sprinkle parsley on top.
4. Serve immediately with pita chips. If your serving dish is deep, use a large spoon to scoop through all seven layers of the dip and serve on individual plates.
5. Serve and enjoy!

Eggplant Parmesan Dip

Ingredients:

2 large eggplants
Olive oil, for drizzling
1 head garlic, top sliced off
1 cup marinara sauce
Kosher salt
Freshly ground black pepper
1/2 cup shredded Parmesan, divided
1 cup shredded mozzarella
1/4 cup packed, fresh basil leaves, plus more for garnish
4 slices low-moisture mozzarella
1/4 cup panko breadcrumbs
1 large French baguette, sliced and toasted

Directions:

1. Preheat oven to 350 degrees F.
2. Line a large baking sheet with foil.
3. Prick eggplants all over and rub with olive oil.
4. Drizzle garlic with olive oil and add to baking sheet.
5. Bake until eggplant is soft and skin is blistered, and garlic is caramelized, 40-45 minutes.
6. Split open eggplants and scoop out flesh.
7. Discard skin.
8. Squeeze out garlic and discard skin as well.
9. Add to food processor along with tomato sauce, salt, pepper, 1/4 cup
10. Parmesan, shredded mozzarella, and basil leaves.
11. Process until smooth.
12. Transfer mixture to medium baking dish and top with sliced mozzarella, remaining Parmesan, then the breadcrumbs.
13. Raise oven to 400 degrees F. Bake until cheese is bubbly and Panko is golden, 20 minutes.
14. Let cool slightly.
15. Garnish with more torn basil and serve with toasted French bread.
16. Serve and enjoy!

Chicken Cordon Bleu Dip

Ingredients:

1 cup shredded Swiss cheese
1 pkg. cream cheese
1 cup ham steak, chopped
1 bag fresh or frozen breaded chicken strips

Directions:

1. Preheat the oven to 425 degrees F.
2. As the oven heats, combine the Swiss, cream cheese and ham in a mixing bowl.
3. Arrange the chicken tenders in a circle in a skillet or oven-safe baking dish, leaving a space in the center for the dip.
4. Spoon in the dip mixture.
5. Bake in the oven for 15-18 minutes, or until the chicken is cooked through and the dip is hot and bubbly.
6. Serve and enjoy!

Mackerel Dip

Ingredients:

1 (15 oz.) can mackerel, drained and rinsed
1 small onion, finely diced
1/4 cup tomato-based hot pepper sauce
2 tsps. salt, or to taste
1 tsp. ground black pepper, or to taste
1 cup mayonnaise

Directions:

1. Remove skin and bones from fish.
2. In a medium bowl, mix fish with onion and hot pepper sauce with a fork, breaking fish into small pieces.
3. Mix in mayonnaise.
4. Season to taste with salt and pepper.
5. Cover, and refrigerate for 2 hours.
6. Serve and enjoy!

Tater Tot Dip

Ingredients:

3 cups tater tots (about 45 whole tater tots), thawed and halved or roughly chopped
1 cup meatballs, crumbled
16 oz. sour cream
2 cups shredded cheese blend, divided (blend of Colby, jack, mozzarella, Monterrey Jack cheese)
2 tsps. all-purpose seasoning blend, or to taste
Salt and pepper to taste

Directions:

1. Preheat oven to 375 degrees F.
2. Spray a 9-inch pie dish or similar oven-safe baking dish with cooking spray; set aside.
3. Slice thawed tater tots in half or place a large pile on cutting board and roughly chop them; retain some size and texture and don't chop them too small.
4. Transfer tater tots to a large mixing bowl.
5. Add the meatballs, sour cream, add 1 cup cheese, seasoning blend, salt, pepper, and stir to combine.
6. 5. Transfer mixture to prepared baking dish, smoothing the top lightly with a spatula.
7. 6. Top with remaining 1 cup cheese.
8. 7. Bake for 30 to 35 minutes, or until top is bubbly and golden browned.
9. 8. Serve and enjoy!

Red Pepper Dip

Ingredients:

16 oz. easy melting cheese (Combine American, Monterrey Jack, Pepper Jack, Havarti, Gruyere, Velveeta, Swiss and/or Cheddar)
1 (4 oz.) pkg. cream cheese
1 (4 oz.) can green chilis
4 oz. chicken, shredded
1 cup diced red bell peppers

Directions:

1. Combine all ingredients in a large microwave-safe bowl, cover with plastic-wrap, and heat on high power to melt, about 3 minutes.
2. Stop and stir and continue to heat in 30-second bursts until cheese has melted can dip can be stirred smooth.
3. Serve and enjoy!

Gorgonzola Dip

Ingredients:

1 cup mayonnaise
1 cup low-fat sour cream
4 oz. Gorgonzola cheese, crumbled
1 tbsp. chopped fresh dill
1 clove garlic, peeled salt and pepper to taste
2 tsps. unflavored gelatin

Directions:

1. In a food processor, place low-fat mayonnaise, low-fat sour cream, Gorgonzola cheese, dill, garlic, salt and pepper.
2. Blend until smooth.
3. Sprinkle gelatin into mixture.
4. Allow it to soften for approximately 5 minutes.
5. Blend to mix in gelatin. Cover and chill in the refrigerator until serving.
6. Serve and enjoy!

Lobster Dip

Ingredients:

1 (7 oz.) can lobster meat, drained and flaked
1 tbsp. minced onion
1 tbsp. lemon juice
1 (8 oz.) pkg. cream cheese, softened
4 tbsps. butter, softened
1 tbsp. prepared horseradish

Directions:

1. In a medium bowl, mix together lobster meat, onion, lemon juice, cream cheese, butter and prepared horseradish.
2. Continue mixing until smooth.
3. Cover and chill in the refrigerator until serving.
4. Serve and enjoy!

Hot Caramelized Onion Dip

Ingredients:

4 bacon strips
2 sweet onions, halved and thinly sliced
1/4 tsp. sugar
1/4 tsp. sea salt
1 tbsp. dry sherry
1/4 tsp. tabasco
1/2 tsp. chopped fresh thyme
1 cup shredded Gruyere Cheese
1/2 cup sour cream
1/2 cup mayo
1/4 tsp. freshly, ground black pepper

Directions:

1. Preheat oven to 400 degrees.
2. Cook bacon in a large nonstick skillet.
3. Remove to a paper towel lined plate to cool.
4. Crumble.
5. Add onions, sugar, and salt to bacon fat in the skillet and cook over medium-high heat for about 5 minutes.
6. Reduce heat to medium and cook, stirring often, until onions turn a deep golden brown color, about 20 minutes.
7. If onions start to burn, turn heat down to medium-low.
8. Add sherry and cook 1 minute. Stir in thyme and tabasco.
9. Remove from heat.
10. Mix together sour cream and mayo in a medium bowl.
11. Add crumbled bacon, cheese, onion mixture, and black pepper. Mix together well and transfer to a 2-cup baking dish.
12. Bake 20 minutes, or until bubbly and golden brown on top.
13. Serve and enjoy!

Lasagne Dip

Ingredients:

8 oz. cream cheese
1 1/2 cup ricotta
3/4 cup grated Parmesan
2 cloves garlic, chopped
1/2 tsp. crushed red pepper flakes
3 cup marinara
1 1/2 cup shredded mozzarella
1 1/2 tsp. fresh oregano, plus more for garnish
Garlic bread or breadsticks, for serving

Directions:

1. In a slow-cooker, combine cream cheese, ricotta, Parmesan, garlic, and crushed red pepper flakes.
2. Stir until combined.
3. Add marinara, mozzarella, and oregano.
4. Cook on high for 1 hour or low for 2 hours, until bubbly.
5. Garnish with oregano and serve with garlic bread or breadsticks.
6. Serve and enjoy!

Banana Pudding Dip

Ingredients:

2 (8-oz) blocks of cream cheese, softened
½ cup powdered sugar
7 oz. sweetened condenses milk
1 cup heavy whipping cream
1 cup prepared instant vanilla pudding
2 bananas
1 tsp. lemon juice
1 box vanilla wafers

Directions:

1. In a small bowl, beat heavy whipping cream until soft peaks form.
2. In another small bowl, prepare pudding according to package instructions.
3. In a large bowl, beat together the cream cheese and powdered sugar until combined.
4. Slowly mix in the condensed milk.
5. Fold 1 cup of the pudding into the cream cheese mixture and then
6. fold in the whipped cream into the mixture
7. On a plate, mash the bananas and sprinkle with lemon juice to help prevent them from browning.
8. 7. Fold bananas into the dip mixture.
9. 8. Chill for an hour and sprinkle the top with crushed vanilla wafers before serving.
10. 9. Serve with vanilla wafers and enjoy!

Bacon Cheeseburger Dip

Ingredients:

1 tbsp. extra-virgin olive oil
1 large onion, chopped
1/2 lb. ground beef
6 slices bacon
8 oz. cream cheese, softened
1 1/2 cup shredded cheddar and Monterey jack
1 tbsp. Worcestershire sauce
1 tsp. garlic powder
Kosher salt
Freshly ground black pepper
Potato chips, for serving

Directions:

1. Preheat oven to 350 degrees F. In a large skillet over medium-high heat, add oil.
2. Cook onions until soft, 4 to 5 minutes, then add beef and cook until no longer pink, 6 to 8 minutes. Transfer to a paper towel-lined plate to soak up grease.
3. Wipe out skillet and add bacon. Cook over medium heat until crispy, about 6 minutes.
4. Transfer to a paper towel-lined plate. Once cool, crumble and transfer to a large bowl.
5. Add cooked hamburger and onions, cream cheese, cheese, Worcestershire, and garlic powder and season with salt and pepper.
6. Transfer mixture to a baking dish and cook until warmed through and cheese is bubbly, 12 to 15 minutes.
7. Serve and enjoy!

Pumpkin Pie Dip

Ingredients:

2 cup heavy cream
1 3.4-oz. instant vanilla pudding mix
1/2 cup canned pumpkin
2 tsp. pumpkin pie spice
Ginger snap cookies, for serving

Directions:

1. In a stand mixer, beat heavy cream and vanilla pudding mix until stiff peaks form, 1 to 2 minutes.
2. Add pumpkin and pumpkin pie spice and stir to combine.
3. Chill if desired.
4. Serve with ginger snaps and enjoy!

Clam Chowder Dip

Ingredients:

1 15-oz. can clam chowder
8 oz. cream cheese, softened
1 cup grated Parmesan
1 clove garlic, minced
Juice of 1/2 lemon
Kosher salt
Freshly ground black pepper
1 boule, top part removed
Dried parsley, for garnish
Saltines, for serving

Directions:

1. Preheat oven to 350 degrees F. In a large bowl, combine clam chowder, cream cheese, Parmesan, garlic, and lemon juice and season with salt and pepper.
2. Transfer mixture to bread bowl and place on a baking sheet.
3. Bake until completely warmed through and bubbly, 20 to 25 minutes.
4. Garnish with dried parsley and serve with Saltines.
5. Serve and enjoy!

Chicken Enchilada Queso Dip

Ingredients:

3 blocks cream cheese (8 oz. each)
2 cup rotisserie chicken breast (or 2 poached chicken breasts), shredded
1 can chopped green chiles
1 1/2 cup shredded Monterey Jack cheese
1 1/2 cup salsa verde
1 tbsp. chopped green onions
1 plum tomato, diced

Directions:

1. Combine all ingredients except green onions and tomato in the slow cooker.
2. Cook on low for 1 1/2 hours, or until everything's melted.
3. Stir and cover with green onions and diced tomatoes before serving.
4. Serve and enjoy!

Chili Mac 'n Cheese Dip

Ingredients:

1 15-oz. can chili con carne
1 large onion, diced
1 cup shredded Mexican cheese
8 oz. cream cheese
1/3 cup lager beer
Few dashes hot sauce
Kosher salt
12 oz. Macaroni
Sour cream, for garnish
Fresh cilantro, for garnish (optional)
Tortilla chips, for serving

Directions:

1. In a small slow-cooker, combine chili, onion, cheese, cream cheese, beer, and hot sauce and heat, covered, on high, 1 hour.
2. Meanwhile, bring a large pot of water to a boil.
3. Season generously with salt and add macaroni.
4. Cook until al dente, 2 minutes, then drain.
5. When ready to serve dip, add macaroni and stir until combined.
6. Garnish with sour cream and cilantro (if using) and serve with tortilla chips.
7. 6. Serve and enjoy!

Meatball Sub Dip

Ingredients:

1/2 a pound of spicy Italian sausage (I used Jennie-O turkey sausage)
16 oz. cream cheese, room temperature
2 1/2 cups shredded mozzarella, divided
2 tsps. dried basil
1 tsp. garlic salt
1 cup of your favorite spaghetti sauce

Directions:

1. Preheat your oven to 375 degrees F.
2. Make small meatballs out of the spicy Italian sausages.
3. In a cast iron skillet over medium heat, add a small amount of olive oil, about a tsp.
4. Cook the mini meatballs, turning them as they brown, until they are fully cooked. Remove them from the skillet and put them on a paper towel lined plate.
5. Pour out any additional oil that remains in the skillet, but no need to clean it.
6. In a large bowl, blend together the cream cheese, basil, garlic salt, and 1/2 cup of the mozzarella cheese until fully combined.
7. Spread it in the bottom of the skillet.
8. Place the meatballs on top, cover with sauce, and then top with the remaining two cups of cheese.
9. Bake for 15 minutes, then turn on the broiler and for five minutes.
10. Keep a close eye on the dip so it doesn't burn.
11. Serve with toasted baguette pieces enjoy!

Mississippi Mud Pie Dip

Ingredients:

1 container cool whip
1 pkg. chocolate pudding mix
1/2 pkg. Oreo cookies
1/3 cup chopped pecans

Directions:

1. Combine Cool Whip and pudding mix in large bowl, beating until all lumps are broken up and batter is fully combined.
2. Place about 9 to 10 Oreos in a gallon-sized re-sealable plastic bag and use rolling pin to crush cookies into a fine crumble.
3. Fold Oreo pieces into batter, along with chopped pecans.
4. Top dip with more crumbled Oreos and pecans.
5. Serve and enjoy!

Bacon Jalapeño Corn Dip

Ingredients:

8 strips bacon
2 (11 oz.) cans whole kernel sweet corn, drained
1 jalapeno, seeded and minced
8 oz. cream cheese, softened
1 cup mozzarella cheese, shredded
½ tsp. salt
Dash of cayenne pepper
¼ cup fresh basil, chopped
Parmesan cheese, to taste

Directions:

1. Preheat oven to 400 degrees F.
2. In a cast iron or ovenproof skillet, cook the bacon over medium heat until slightly crispy.
3. Remove from heat and set on paper towels to absorb excess grease.
4. Drain off all but 1 tsp. of the grease remaining in the pan.
5. Use the bacon grease to grease the pan.
6. Crumble the bacon.
7. Combine the corn, jalapeno, cream cheese, mozzarella, salt, cayenne, half of the bacon, and half of the basil.
8. Scoop into the skillet and bake for 20 minutes.
9. Sprinkle with the remaining bacon and basil, and parmesan cheese to taste.
10. Serve and enjoy!

Red Velvet Cake Batter Dip

Ingredients:

1 block cream cheese (8 oz.), softened
1 cup frozen whipped topping, like Cool Whip
3/4 cup red velvet cake mix
1/2 cup mini white chocolate chips
1 pkg. graham crackers, for dipping

Directions:

1. Beat cream cheese using an electric mixer until it's light and fluffy.
2. Turn the mixer to low and add in the whipped topping and red velvet cake mix.
3. Once thoroughly combined, turn off the mixer and use a silicone spatula or spoon to fold in the white chocolate chips.
4. Serve with graham crackers or chocolate wafers for dipping.
5. Serve and enjoy!

Chili Cheese Dog Dip

Pigs in a Blanket Ingredients:

1 tube Crescent roll dough
1 pkg. cocktail wieners
Olive oil for brushing dough

Dip Ingredients:

1 (8 oz.) pkg. cream cheese
1 can Chili
1 cup cheddar cheese, plus more for topping
Diced scallions

Directions:

1. Preheat the oven to 350 degrees F.
2. Unroll Crescent roll dough and cut each triangle into three slices.
3. Roll a slice around each cocktail wieners, forming a Pig in a Blanket.
4. Place each Pig in a Blanket side-by-side in a skillet, forming a wreath shape.
5. Brush the top of each one with olive oil.
6. In a medium-sized bowl, mix cream cheese, chili and cheddar.
7. Pour mixture into center of wreath.
8. Sprinkle the top of the dip with extra cheese.
9. Bake for 20 minutes, or until the dip is bubbly and the cheese has melted.
10. Top dip with diced scallions and let cool for 5-7 minutes before serving.
11. Serve and enjoy!

Beef Enchilada Dip

Ingredients:

2 pounds ground beef
1/2 medium onion, diced
2 cloves garlic, minced
2 cups enchilada sauce
2 cups grated Monterrey Jack or cheddar cheese
Sour Cream (optional)
Tortilla Chips (optional)

Directions:

1. Brown ground beef in a large skillet.
2. Drain. Add in onion and garlic and cook until tender, about 3 minutes.
3. Stir in enchilada sauce and top with grated cheese.
4. Cover and allow cheese to melt, about 3 more minutes.
5. Top with sour cream and serve with tortilla chips.
6. Serve and enjoy!

Bacon Asparagus Dip

Ingredients:

1 bunch asparagus, trimmed and roughly chopped
1 tbsp. extra-virgin olive oil
Kosher salt
Freshly ground black pepper
4 slices cooked bacon
2 oz. softened cream cheese (1/4 block)
1 cup shredded sharp white cheddar
1/2 cup shredded Gruyere
1/2 cup sour cream
1/4 cup Chopped chives
Freshly ground black pepper

Directions:

1. Heat broiler.
2. On a baking sheet, toss asparagus with olive oil and season with salt and pepper.
3. Broil until tender and slightly charred, 5 to 7 minutes.
4. Reduce heat to 375 degrees F.
5. Transfer asparagus to a large bowl.
6. Add chopped bacon, cream cheese, cheddar, gruyere, and chives and season with black pepper.
7. Stir until combined.
8. Transfer dip to a bread bowl or baking dish and bake until cheese is bubbly and dip warmed through, 15 to 20 minutes.
9. Serve with bread, crackers, or vegetables and enjoy!

Kentucky Hot Brown Dip

Ingredients:

8 oz. cream cheese, at room temperature
¼ cup plain Greek yogurt (I used nonfat)
¼ tsp. grated nutmeg
1 1/2 cups shredded cheddar cheese, divided
2 cups chopped cooked turkey
1 small tomato, seeded and chopped
6 slices bacon, crumbled
1/4 cup grated parmesan cheese
Crackers, sliced baguette, vegetables for serving

Directions:

1. Preheat oven to 350 degrees F.
2. In a bowl, stir together the cream cheese, yogurt, nutmeg, 1 cup cheddar, and turkey until thoroughly combined.
3. Transfer to a glass baking dish and spread evenly.
4. Top with tomato, bacon, the remaining 2 oz. cheddar cheese, and the pecorino romano cheese.
5. Bake at 350°F for about 30 minutes, or until hot and bubbly, and lightly browned.
6. Serve with crackers, baguette slices, and veggies for dipping.
7. Serve and enjoy!

Toffee Apple Dip

Ingredients:

1 (8 oz.) pkg. cream cheese, softened
3/4 cup packed light-brown sugar
1 (8 oz.) pkg. toffee bits

Directions:

1. In a mixing bowl using an electric hand mixer, whip together cream cheese with brown sugar until smooth and fluffy, about 1 minute.
2. Reserve 1 tbsp. toffee bits then fold in remainder.
3. Transfer to a serving bowl.
4. Sprinkle top with remaining 1 toffee bits.
5. Serve with apple slices and enjoy!

Snickers Dip

Ingredients:

4 Snickers candy bars
4 oz. cream cheese
1 cup Cool Whip
1 tbsp. peanut butter

Directions:

1. Break the Snickers candy bars into bite size pieces
2. Add Snickers, cream cheese, Cool Whip and peanut butter to an
3. electric mixer
4. Mix on medium speed for 30 seconds
5. Place into serving dish and enjoy!
6. Serve and enjoy!

Coconut Caramel Cookie Dip

Ingredients:

8 oz. soft Philly cream cheese
8 oz. cool whip
½ cup powdered sugar
2 tbsp. caramel sauce
1 cup toasted coconut
Chocolate sauce
Jar of caramel sauce for topping

Directions:

1. Preheat oven to 375 degrees F.
2. Lay coconut on a cookie sheet and cook 5-8 mins until golden.
3. Watch closely.
4. In a mixer, beat cream cheese, sugar, caramel and cool whip until blended.
5. Pour into a ramekin or bowl.
6. Top with the toasted coconut.
7. Drizzle on lots of chocolate and caramel sauces.
8. Serve with cookies/graham crackers.
9. Serve and enjoy!

Shrimp Scampi Dip

Ingredients:

2 tbsps. unsalted butter
8 oz. medium shrimp, peeled, deveined and roughly chopped
4 garlic cloves, minced
½ tsp. red pepper flakes
¼ cup white wine
2 tbsps. lemon juice
salt and pepper (to taste)
4 oz. cream cheese, at room temperature
¼ cup sour cream
3 tbsps. mayonnaise
½ cup shredded mozzarella cheese, divided
2 tbsps. grated parmesan cheese

Directions:

1. Preheat oven to 350 degrees F.
2. Lightly oil a 9-inch baking dish or coat with nonstick spray.
3. Melt butter in a large skillet over medium high heat. Add shrimp, garlic and red pepper flakes.
4. Cook, stirring occasionally, until pink, about 2 minutes.
5. Stir in wine and lemon juice; season with salt and pepper, to taste.
6. Bring to a simmer; remove from heat and stir in cream cheese, sour cream, mayonnaise, parsley, 1/4 cup mozzarella and Parmesan.
7. Spread mixture into the prepared baking dish; sprinkle with remaining 1/4 cup mozzarella.
8. Place into oven and bake until bubbly and golden, about 10-12 minutes.
9. Serve and enjoy!

Hot Fudge Sundae Dip

Ingredients:

1 container frozen whipped topping
1 pkg. vanilla pudding mix
1 banana sliced
Chocolate fudge sauce
Rainbow sprinkles
Maraschino cherry, for garnish

Directions:

1. Combine whipped topping, pudding mix and half of the banana slices in a large mixing bowl.
2. Use an electric mixer to beat ingredients together until thoroughly combined.
3. Fold in about one tbsp. of fudge sauce, mixing it just enough to create ribbons of fudge—not completely stirring it in.
4. Top the dip with banana slices, sprinkles and a fudge drizzle.
5. Add a cherry on top.
6. Serve and enjoy!

Cinnamon Roll Cheesecake Dip

Ingredients:

1 pkg. cream cheese
1/4 cup powdered sugar
2 tsp. cinnamon, divided
2 tbsp. butter, melted
2 tsp. sugar

Directions:

1. Combine cream cheese, powdered sugar and 1 tsp. cinnamon in a medium-sized bowl. Beat with a whisk or silicone spatula until the mixture is light, fluffy and no longer lumpy (about 2-3 minutes).
2. In a separate bowl, combine remaining cinnamon, melted butter and sugar.
3. Mix to combine.
4. Pour this mixture into the cream cheese batter, folding it in just enough to create cinnamon-sugar swirls in the dip.
5. Serve with graham crackers or apple slices.
6. Serve and enjoy!

Black Bean Dip

Ingredients:

1 can (15 oz.) black beans, rinsed
1/2 cup Miracle Whip salad dressing
1/2 cup Sour cream
1 can (4 oz.) chopped green chiles, drained
2 Tbsp. chopped cilantro
1 tsp. garlic powder
Few drops hot pepper sauce

Directions:

1. Mix all ingredients until well blended.
2. Refrigerate several hours or until chilled.
3. Serve with crackers or assorted fresh vegetable dippers.
4. Serve and enjoy!

Pasta Sauce Chip Dip

Ingredients:

Sour cream
Pasta sauce
Grated Parmesan cheese, to taste
Ground pepper, to taste
Oregano, to taste

Directions:

1. Combine equal parts sour cream and pasta sauce in a bowl.
2. Stir in Parmesan cheese, pepper and oregano.
3. Serve with chips and enjoy!

Italian Veggie Dip

Ingredients:

1 small eggplant, chopped
1 cup chopped onions
1 cup chopped red peppers
2 cloves garlic, minced
1/4 cup sun dried tomato vinaigrette dressing
1 zucchini, chopped
1 large tomato, chopped
1/4 cup grated Parmesan cheese
1/2 cup shredded Mozzarella cheese
Multi-grain toasted chips

Directions:

1. Cook and stir eggplant, onions, peppers and garlic in dressing in large skillet on medium heat 8 min.
2. Stir in zucchini and tomatoes; cover. Simmer 5 to 7 min. or until tender.
3. Stir in Parmesan cheese.
4. Spoon into serving bowl.
5. Sprinkle with mozzarella cheese.
6. Serve with chips and enjoy!

Ranch Dressing Dip

Ingredients:

3/4 cup sour cream
1/2 cup mayonnaise
1/3 cup chopped fresh flat-leaf parsley
1/4 cup chopped fresh chives
1/4 tsp. minced garlic
1/4 tsp. salt
1/4 tsp. black pepper
4 carrots, cut into sticks
6 celery ribs, cut into sticks
1 seedless cucumber (usually plastic-wrapped), cut into sticks
1 small jicama, peeled, halved lengthwise, and cut into sticks
1 1/2 cups grape or cherry tomatoes (9 oz.)

Directions:

1. Stir together sour cream, mayonnaise, parsley, chives, garlic, salt, and pepper in a bowl until combined well.
2. Chill dip, covered, until slightly thickened, at least 1 hour (for flavors to develop).
3. Serve dip with vegetables.

French Onion Dip

Ingredients:

2 tbsps. olive oil
1 1/2 cups chopped onion
1/4 tsp. kosher salt 1 cup sour cream
1 cup mayonnaise
1/2 tsp. garlic powder
1/4 tsp. ground white pepper
1/2 tsp. kosher salt

Directions:

1. Heat the oil in a large skillet over medium heat; add the onions and 1/4 tsp. of kosher salt.
2. Cook and stir until the onions are caramelized to a nice golden brown, about 20 minutes.
3. Remove the onions from the heat and cool.
4. Mix together the sour cream, mayonnaise, garlic powder, white pepper, and remaining kosher salt. Stir in the onions when they are cool.
5. Cover and refrigerate the dip for at least 2 hours before serving.

About the Author

Laura Sommers is **The Recipe Lady!**

She is a loving wife and mother who lives on a small farm in Baltimore County, Maryland and has a passion for all things domestic especially when it comes to saving money. She has a profitable eBay business and is a couponing addict. Follow her tips and tricks to learn how to make delicious meals on a budget, save money or to learn the latest life hack!

Visit her Amazon Author Page to see her latest books:

amazon.com/author/laurasommers

Visit the Recipe Lady's blog for even more great recipes and to learn which books are **FREE** for download each week:

http://the-recipe-lady.blogspot.com/

Follow the Recipe Lady on **Pinterest**:

http://pinterest.com/therecipelady1

Subscribe to The Recipe Lady blog through Amazon and have recipes and updates sent directly to your Kindle:

The Recipe Lady Blog through Amazon

Laura Sommers is also an Extreme Couponer and Penny Hauler! If you would like to find out how to get things for **FREE** with coupons or how to get things for only a **PENNY**, then visit her couponing blog **Penny Items and Freebies**

http://penny-items-and-freebies.blogspot.com/

Other books by Laura Sommers

- **Recipes for Chicken Wings**
- **50 Super Awesome Salsa Recipes!**
- **Super Summer Barbecue and Pool Party Picnic Salad Recipes!**
- **50 Super Awesome Coleslaw and Potato Salad Recipes**
- **Homemade Salad Dressing Recipes from Scratch!**
- **50 Super Awesome Pasta Salad Recipes!**
- **50 Delicious Homemade Ice Cream Recipes**

May all of your meals be a banquet
with good friends and good food.

Made in the USA
Middletown, DE
12 May 2022